First Facts®

Snakes

Corn Snakes

by Van Wallach

Consultant:
Robert T. Mason, PhD
Professor of Zoology
J.C. Braly Curator of Vertebrates
Oregon State University, Corvallis

Capstone
press®

Mankato, Minnesota

First Facts is published by Capstone Press,
151 Good Counsel Drive, P.O. Box 669, Mankato, Minnesota 56002.
www.capstonepress.com

Library of Congress Cataloging-in-Publication Data
Wallach, V. (Van)
    Corn snakes / Van Wallach.
    p. cm. — (First facts. Snakes)
    Includes bibliographical references and index.
    Summary: "A brief introduction to corn snakes, including their habitat, food,
and life cycle"— Provided by publisher.
    ISBN-13: 978-1-4296-2272-1 (hardcover)
    ISBN-10: 1-4296-2272-5 (hardcover)
    1. Corn snake — Juvenile literature. I. Title. II. Series.
QL666.O636W34 2009
597.96'2 — dc22
                                                  2008028703

Editorial Credits

Lori Shores, editor; Ted Williams, designer and illustrator; Danielle Ceminsky, illustrator;
    Jo Miller, photo researcher

Photo Credits

Bruce Coleman Inc./Daniel J. Lyons, 16; Jeff A. Cole, 10; John Bell, 21; John Giustina, 20
Corbis/David A. Northcott, 18
iStockphoto/Eric Isselee, cover, 1
Jupiterimages Corporation, 4–5
Peter Arnold/John R. MacGregor, 12–13; WILDLIFE, 15
Photo Researchers Inc/Dan Suzio, 9
Visuals Unlimited/David G. Campbell, 6

Essential content terms are **bold** and are defined at the bottom of the page
where they first appear.

1 2 3 4 5 6 14 13 12 11 10 09

Table of Contents

The Red Rat Snake

Corn snakes are sometimes called red rat snakes. But corn snakes in the wild are usually orange. They have large spots or blotches on their bodies. These marks can be red, yellow, or orange.

Fun Fact!
Corn snakes' bellies are white with black squares. Their bellies look like checkerboards.

spear-shaped marking

From Head to Scale

You can remember a corn snake by its markings. Corn snakes have spear-shaped markings on top of their heads.

Like all reptiles, corn snakes are covered with **scales**. The scales on a corn snake's belly are square with sharp corners.

Fun Fact!

Most corn snakes are 3 to 4 feet (1 to 1.2 meters) long. The longest corn snake was 6 feet (1.8 meters) long.

scale: a piece of hard, dry skin

Corn Snake Range

□ where corn snakes live

North America

Europe

Asia

Africa

South America

Australia

Antarctica

N · W · E · S

Home Sweet Home

Corn snakes live in the eastern United States. They are found in lowland areas, like meadows and rocky hillsides.

8

Corn snakes also live in forests. They live mainly on the ground, but they are also good climbers. Corn snakes can climb straight up the side of a tree.

On the Hunt

Corn snakes are sneaky hunters. They crawl through **burrows** looking for **prey**. Corn snakes also hunt for rats and mice in barns and empty buildings.

Corn snakes use their sense of smell to find prey. They flick their tongues out to pick up scents from the air. A special organ in the snake's mouth identifies the smells.

Fun Fact!
Corn snakes are nocturnal, which means they are active at night.

burrow: a hole in the ground where an animal lives
prey: an animal hunted by an another animal for food

A Tight Squeeze

A corn snake **constricts** animals before eating them. The snake wraps its strong body around its prey. Then the snake squeezes tighter and tighter until the animal stops breathing.

Fun Fact!
If given a dead mouse, a corn snake will still squeeze it before eating.

constrict: to squeeze tightly to prevent breathing   13

Dinnertime

Snakes can eat any animal that fits into their mouths. But corn snakes like mice and baby rats the best. They also eat small birds and eggs.

Corn snakes swallow their prey whole. Their jaws are stretchy and can open very wide. Their skin also stretches to make room for a big meal.

Fun Fact!

Corn snakes never eat more than once each week. They can go months without eating at all.

Life Cycle of a Corn Snake

Newborn

Baby corn snakes use an egg tooth to cut through their shells.

Young

Young corn snakes eat small lizards and frogs.

Newborn

Adult

Corn snakes are ready to mate in one to two years.

Snake Eggs

Male and female corn snakes mate in the spring. Then the female lays a **clutch** of three to 40 eggs. She hides the clutch in a rotting stump or animal burrow. These areas keep the eggs safe and warm.

Fun Fact!
Snake eggs are not hard like chicken eggs. They are soft like leather.

clutch: a group of eggs laid at the same time

Growing Up

The baby snakes grow in their eggs for about 45 days. They hatch in late summer. Newborn corn snakes are only 6 to 14 inches (15 to 36 centimeters) long. They are easy targets for **predators**, like birds and raccoons. Sometimes only a few snakes from one clutch will grow into adults.

Fun Fact!
One out of every 5,000 corn snakes is born with two heads!

---

predator: an animal that hunts other animals for food

Living Long

In the wild, corn snakes face many dangers. But corn snakes can live for many years in **<u>captivity</u>**. At one zoo, a corn snake lived for 20 years.

captivity: the condition of being kept in a cage

Amazing but True!

Corn snakes are popular pets. They are easy to tame, and rarely bite. Snake breeders have developed corn snakes with more than 50 different color patterns. Some are white, and others are charcoal gray. Some corn snakes are even purple!

Glossary

burrow (BUHR-oh) — a tunnel or hole in the ground where an animal lives

captivity (kap-TIV-ih-tee) — the condition of being kept in a cage

clutch (KLUHCH) — a group of eggs laid by a single female

constrict (kuhn-STRIKT) — to squeeze tightly to limit or prevent breathing

predator (PRED-uh-tur) — an animal that hunts other animals for food

prey (PRAY) — an animal hunted by another animal for food

scale (SKALE) — one of the small pieces of hard skin that cover the body of a fish or reptile

Read More

Christiansen, Per. *Constrictor Snakes.* Nature's Monsters. Pleasantville, N.Y.: Gareth Stevens, 2008.

Feeney, Kathy. *Caring for Your Snake.* Positively Pets. Mankato, Minn.: Capstone Press, 2008.

Hughes, Monica. *Scary Snakes.* I Love Reading. New York: Bearport, 2006.

Internet Sites

FactHound offers a safe, fun way to find educator-approved Internet sites related to this book.

Here's what you do:

1. Visit *www.facthound.com*
2. Choose your grade level.
3. Begin your search.

This book's ID number is 9781429622721.

FactHound will fetch the best sites for you!

Index